PRAISE FOR JOU

MW00852255

"Thank you, Kamin, for sharing this inspirational story. *Journey to Abundance* is a beacon of hope and light, and I know it will be a tremendous guide for people who find themselves in situations similar to yours."
~ Karrie L. Klassen, MA
Klassen Marketing
www.klassenmarketing.com

"Kamin's heartfelt personal story combined with her laser-focused and thought-provoking questions and activities will change your perspective about money, wealth and abundance. If you follow all the activities she presents your life will definitely improve. If you have any issues with money, you need this book!"
~ Felicia J. Slattery, MA, MAdEd
Communication Consultant & Speaker
www.communicationtransformation.com

"Kamin speaks from the heart. She does it with such love and complete honesty that you cannot help but to learn from it. Since implementing just one of the ideas in her book, my business has taken a turn towards even more abundance. I have posted a little mantra in front of me on my desk. Real estate transactions fraught with challenges, have since closed gracefully. There is even an immediate effect that I experience. My shoulders seem to relax and tension melts away when I recall these simple words. My mantra is not exactly the same as the ones that Kamin describes in her book, but that is part of the power in her message. Kamin reminds us that there is power within us to make a difference in our own lives, and that once we kindle it in our own personal way, we can reach any goal."

~ Laura Holder
Real Estate Broker

"Through sharing her moving, personal story, Kamin Bell demonstrates what strength of heart really means. Her authentic book, *Journey to Abundance*, is guaranteed to touch hearts, and help those facing financial challenges to live a more abundant life."

~ Vickie Woods, MA
MFT Intern

"Through *Journey to Abundance* I learned how to use mantras and set clear intentions. And, I learned the power of forgiveness and healing. This book is a wonderful tool to lead you to your journey towards abundance!"

~ Lisa Martina Head
Insurance Agent

"*Journey to Abundance* is a story that real people can relate to. Kamin was successful in many ways, but she made some bad choices and lost a lot of money and things before she learned how to embrace abundance. She shares it all here, boldly and honestly, warts and all. As you read along, you'll be shaking your head at some of her choices, grimacing when she stumbles, and rooting for her with each step towards a new relationship to abundance. There are no 'get rich quick' tips here. These are lessons and principles that anyone can apply to achieve an affluent life of abundance - having all that you need and being able to get what you truly want."

~ Steve Coxsey
Personal Growth Coach
www.SteveCoxsey.com

"Kamin exemplifies what it means to be a successful woman and possesses that unique ability to overcome life's challenges with grace and humility. From reading *Journey to Abundance*, both women and men stand to gain greater insight into their own opportunities for success and, more importantly, the infinite potential that awaits anyone willing to take action and responsibility for their future. Keep your eye on Kamin - At this pace, she will be another hero and role model for a modern generation of aspiring women and men."

~ Uday
Founder & CEO
Live on Campus

"I love this book! Kamin has written an inspiring book, using her own vulnerability and courage to help her readers on their *Journey to Abundance*. She has included a wealth of resources, quotes, and questions within this book to help the reader dig deep and to create their own success plan. This book will help you get on the road to prosperity and stay there!"

~ Karen L. Rose, MA
Professional Speaker & Author
www.KarenRoseSpeaker.com

"With wit, wisdom and effortless grace, Kamin welcomes you into her world and shares her extraordinary story of courage, of challenge and of triumph. Combining sound financial strategy with the art and science of conscious creation, this work is a must-read for all who want to live a better life. For all who are searching for hope, in your finances and in your life, your journey has wisely led your here."

~ Brian Evans, MA, MBA
Author, Speaker & Coach
www.Inspiriteur.com

Journey to

ABUNDANCE

Journey to
ABUNDANCE

A Workbook and Resource Guide for Creating the Prosperous Life You Desire

———◆◆◆———

KAMIN A. BELL, MS, MA

WORDS HAVE LIFE
P R E S S
Aliso Viejo, California

Words Have Life Press
26895 Aliso Creek Road, Suite B289
Aliso Viejo, CA, 92656, USA

Cover artwork by Jody Bergsma, www.bergsma.com.
Used by permission of Bergsma Gallery Press. All rights reserved.

Cover design by Cyanotype Book Architects, www.cyanotype.ca.

Edited by Linda Dessau, www.lindadessau.com.

Author photograph by Judy Alexander,
www.judyalexanderphotography.com.

Publisher's Cataloging-In-Publication Data
Bell, Kamin A.
   Journey to abundance : a workbook and resource guide for creating the prosperous life you desire / Kamin A. Bell.
     p. ; cm.

   Includes bibliographical references.
   ISBN: 978-0-9800223-2-2 (pbk.)
   ISBN: 978-0-9800223-0-8 (eBook)

1. Self-actualization (Psychology)--Religious aspects--Handbooks, manuals, etc.. 2. Self-help techniques. 3. Wealth. 4. Success--Religious aspects. 5. Finance, Personal--Miscellanea. I. Title.

BF637.S4 B45 2007
158.1   2007938837

Printed in the United States of America
10 9 8 7 6 5 4 3 2

To My Parents,
For all your love and support.

To Reverend Diane Harmony,
For giving me hope and showing me the way.

a•bun•dance

1. A great or plentiful amount.
2. Fullness to overflowing: "My thoughts... are from the abundance of my heart" (Thomas De Quincey).
3. Affluence; wealth

Table of Contents

ACKNOWLEDGMENTS

From the depth of my heart, I am grateful to so many who have been on this journey with me and have enriched my life immeasurably.

I thank God first and foremost for giving me the strength and courage to live through, survive, thrive and tell my story. Thank you for grace and mercy and for ALWAYS being there. I love you.

I thank Drs Ron and Mary Hulnick and the staff at the University of Santa Monica for creating such a wonderful program that gave me tools and techniques to learn from so I could heal and share my life more fully. I am grateful to my project team, Gina Ryan, Greg Voisen, and Joe Granata, and all of my classmates for their loving support and encouragement as I moved my thoughts to form.

To Vickie Woods, thank you for holding my virtual hand, encouraging and inspiring me and for listening and nurturing me throughout this project. Additionally, the love and support from you, Mary Thomson and Masako Stewart has filled my life and my heart with so much joy and love. I thank and love you all.

Thank you Katie Aaron, for your love and friendship and for all of your prayers throughout the years. You are such an amazing blessing in my life.

Felicia Slattery, I so appreciate your coaching and collaboration to create and meet milestones that moved this project and me forward. Thank you.

To CDR Susan Yoshihara, PhD (Ret) and CDR Arlene Shoults: thank you for your friendship and encouragement through the years. You truly inspire me.

I am so grateful to my parents, Robert and Marion, for your loving guidance, support and prayers throughout my life. Thank you also to Kelvin, Kristie, and Keane and their spouses and amazing children. Your love means the world to me.

Thank you Reverend Diane Harmony, for being a guiding light of what is possible through Spirit. Thank you for birthing *5 Gifts for an Abundant Life* so we all might live and experience more abundance in every area of our lives.

I am grateful to Kenneth Copeland Ministries, and the affiliated ministries, for teaching me Biblical principles of abundance and prosperity.

Thank you Dr. Roger and Susan Crenshaw, for your generosity, care and support as I worked to improve my circumstances.

Barbara Winter, thank you for your commitment to showing the world that being an entrepreneur can be joyful.

Thank you Valerie Young for your inspiration and mentoring that facilitated me releasing this book into the world. I also thank you and the Fast Track community for your encouragement to live my dreams.

Oprah Winfrey, thank you for your commitment to teaching and sharing your passion for personal growth for over twenty years. Your "Spirit" segments years ago helped move me to higher ground. And, your "Debt Diet" segments encouraged me to finish this book and share my story. I am truly grateful.

To those who made this book beautiful: Linda Dessau, thank you so much for your gifted editing and shaping of *Journey*. Thank you Jody Bergsma for creating such a beautiful design that captured my vision, even though you didn't know me. And, Sarah Van Male, thank you for such a beautiful cover design.

Kathryn Hall, our writing lunches gave me permission to write and dream. Thank you for your friendship and for helping me make my writing a priority.

To Lindsay MacLean, Beth Hettig and Michael Nussbaum, thank you for your creative input and support as I completed this project. And, to all of my teams over the years, thank you for blessing me so richly and allowing me to coach and guide you on your journey.

I am grateful for all of the reviewers of this book. I truly appreciate your time, effort and acknowledgement of this work.

I am thankful also to you, my reader, for your willingness to read my story and see new possibilities for your own life.

How to Use This Book

The themes of my journey criss-cross through my chronological experience, so that's the way I've presented them here. I'll remind you where we are in my journey as we're discussing each theme, and there is a timeline of significant events for your reference in Appendix C.

I encourage you to take the time to fill the spaces I've provided at the end of each chapter in the *Your Journey* sections, with your own thoughts and exploration of your process. By doing these exercises, you will further your own JOURNEY TO ABUNDANCE.

WELCOME

I don't know where you are on your journey. You may be in a little debt or a lot, so much so that you are having difficulty sleeping and even breathing. I know what that's like and I know how difficult it was for me. It may be difficult to even believe there is a light at the end of the tunnel, let alone visualize one. If this is where you are, I ask you to hang in there with me on this journey to discover the power that exists within you to get free and breathe effortlessly. If you have little or no debt and are just looking to enhance your situation, welcome. You will find ways to avoid the path that I took and grow to even greater prosperity.

Now, I need to tell you that this story involves God. It involves a very personal relationship I have with God. However, I will not preach to you. This book isn't about doctrine or religion but is a spiritual quest to know God and find out what He wants for my life. There are Bible verses I used along my journey that I will share with you. And, there are other spiritual and self-help teachings I will pass on as well. If you don't believe there is a God or Higher Power then consider this: you only have yourself to get you out of this situation and you are the same person who got you into it.

Whatever your beliefs, I ask you to suspend disbelief for the duration of this book and continue reading. You may discover some tools along the way that you can shape to your situation and use to make progress in your life. If you are angry at God or feel that He has abandoned you, definitely keep reading. I felt the same way and you'll learn from my life how I reconciled those feelings. If you already have a close personal relationship with God, you may find that mine is quite different from yours. In all of these scenarios, wherever you are, that is okay.

The God that I serve, in my opinion, is a kind and loving God with a great sense of humor. And for the record, I come from a Christian background and I believe there is only one God, called by many names. If the word God has a negative connotation for you, feel free to substitute whatever name soothes your soul: Higher Power, The One, Jehovah, Spirit, etc. My God happens to be a He. Yours may be a He, She, or It. Whatever works best for you is fine for this journey. I simply ask that if you want greater prosperity, more joy, and more peace, suspend all disbelief for this short journey and discover for yourself your own truth.

My greatest wish is that you or someone you know, might find even a small ray of hope through reading my story. I have said that if I help just one person from going to the depths I went to, it will have all been worth it. I've had the opportunity to help a number of people listen more to their hearts and believe in themselves to gain more abundance. I'd like to help you as well.

I must caution you, however. This is not a get-rich-quick scheme and I will not show you how to make a million dollars next year. Getting to a place of abundance has been a journey that has taken years. And, while I'm not a millionaire, I live a wonderful and comfortable lifestyle. You must choose your own standards, and you simply must do the inner work that's necessary for this journey. I have great peace and I work at that every day. So while you may want to be rich tomorrow, and it could happen, in this book what I will show you are practical steps you can take to get some breathing room, take control of your life, and create a life of abundance.

My friend, come join me on my journey and begin your own precious journey to experiencing greater abundance in your own life.

WORDS HAVE LIFE

And, thoughts are things.

There have been times when I wished I had a true rags-to-riches story, but I don't. There have been countless stories of those that were born into poverty and raised themselves to great stature and/or wealth like Oprah Winfrey, Wayne Dyer, and those in the Horatio Alger Association. I thought maybe if I had been born poor there would have been some fight in me; that bit of scrappiness that they all seemed to possess, that drive to leave their meager beginnings behind them.

You see, I was seemingly one of the lucky ones. I was born to well-educated, upper-middle class African-American parents who lived in a predominantly white Maryland suburb of Washington, D.C. I went to great schools and lived amongst affluence. 6000+-square-foot homes were the norm. We had housekeepers and very nice material possessions. We skied and traveled to wonderful places.

When I joined the U.S. Navy in 1985 after college, I became the Navy's first African-American female helicopter pilot and seemingly had it all. I was able to buy houses, travel overseas, and even get my first masters degree, going to school fulltime with full pay and benefits. My rank commanded respect and afforded me remarkable opportunities. However, by about the eight-year mark, I began to want out. I felt trapped and like a square peg in a round hole. When I had joined the service, I had been far more enamored with being a Naval officer than a pilot. Becoming a Naval Aviator was a choice I made as I graduated from college. I called it "an adult decision," far different from my male counterparts who had all wanted to fly since they were five years old. I remember one of them saying, "I don't think there's anything else I could do but fly." That struck something deep within me since what I was doing wasn't something I always wanted to do. I knew I could do more than fly and I had to prove it to myself and the world.

I was hungry for anything to come along and save me from my life. I was tired of being one of the boys. I so wanted to be a girl, to make a difference, and to have more freedom and money. I wanted to prove I could do anything. About that time, I joined a sales organization for women. I need to be clear here that it was not the organization or type of business that got me into my financial mess. I was hungry for attention, recognition, and to be a girl. They just happened to be the vehicle. I didn't go broke because of the business I chose. I went there because of a few words that I spoke aloud and the imaginations of my mind, the things I dwelt upon. I went broke because of my beliefs.

It was September of 1994 and my last day in the military. I had served nine years as a Naval Aviator, and I had gone to the disbursing (payroll) office to pick up my final paycheck. I had saved up almost two months of vacation to be paid out. However, when I arrived they told me that it had been recouped because I was leaving my contract early. I was devastated. I had expected well over $5,000. That money was to carry me through my first months on my own. Sitting there in the office these words came out of my mouth, "I had planned on that money. I'll have to file bankruptcy without it."

I don't recall thinking about that prior to my going in to pick up my check. I knew I was a bit overextended, but for whatever reason that day, I said those words from the core of my being with great feeling. I honestly didn't know what I was going to do. I panicked and those words began playing over and over again in my head, paralyzing me with fear and preventing me from moving forward. I was so frightened. My worst-case scenario of filing for bankruptcy and losing my two homes played continuously in my head for over a year until I had no other choice.

I had intended to become a million dollar sales person and make my mark on the world. However, repeating, "I'm going to have to file bankruptcy" in my head prevented me from making the kind of sales I wanted and needed to make. I found myself looking at potential new clients not as friends I hadn't met yet, but as food. Nothing good comes from that approach. I bargained with and even threatened myself to get out there and sell more, but nothing worked while that predominant thought was screaming at me. When people around me asked how things were going I looked them straight in the eye and lied that everything was great. I was so embarrassed that I'd left an amazing career to do something I was failing at.

As the months wore on, I got deeper and deeper in debt using my credit cards to sustain my business. I also got more and more silent. Shame and anguish ruled my inner thoughts. A principal lesson I remember my parents repeating to me as I grew up was never to file bankruptcy. Nothing much else was said about it, but it clearly stuck with me, and here I was doing the one thing they told me never to do. How could I ask them for help knowing how much I would disappoint them?

I filed for bankruptcy in November 1995, 14 months after I left the service. I was devastated and embarrassed, yet I was still doing my sales job and holding motivational meetings, even though I was dying inside. I berated myself almost every waking moment with shoulds and should haves.

In the months that followed the filing, the silence grew louder as more of my fears of being alone and homeless came to the forefront. I grabbed on to one get-rich scheme after another. I got whatever self-help books I could get. Silence became my friend, as did my books. Creditors had been calling so I turned off my ringer. I stopped answering the door. It was just me, my thoughts and God in the house. I prayed and prayed for God to miraculously get me through my troubles. That someone would stop by with a big check or I'd win the lottery (though I never played). I fantasized that I had become successful in sales. The pain was excruciating and the silence deafening.

As I mentioned earlier, I wish that I'd been scrappier, a fighter. Instead, I found myself paralyzed with fear. You may be saying, "Why didn't you just get a job to make ends meet?" I asked myself that question so many times. I believe it had to do with admitting defeat, quitting. I continuously held out hope for something to change miraculously. There were so many things, in hindsight, that I could have done to prevent the bankruptcy, but pride also stood in the way. I could have gotten a job to make ends meet, but what if someone saw me working at a department store? True, I had a master's degree and might have been able to get a high paying job, but my self-esteem was so low by that point, my degrees didn't matter. I couldn't bear to be seen by someone who knew me and what I'd been before – a pilot and a sales director. You see, I identified who I was with what I did as a profession and I was painfully aware just how far I'd fallen. A part of me also thought that if I just believed enough or begged God enough, I'd be saved. Another reason I didn't get a job was denial. I just couldn't believe I would lose everything. And at that time, it was truly a full-time job just to breathe. I wasn't sure I could survive the mess I'd gotten myself into.

It was March 1996 and I was once again faced with my thoughts. Within two days, I received the bankruptcy discharge, the foreclosure notices for both houses, and an IRS audit notice. My breathing almost immediately ceased when I read the IRS letter. The religious saying that God doesn't give you more than you can handle was ever present in my mind. I felt that statement was a lie, and I told God so. I felt like the biblical figure Job, when he lost everything and was tempted to turn away from God. I wasn't sure I'd persevere. It was just too much.

About that time, I remember standing in my kitchen one day scanning the room. The weight of the debt had become too much. As I looked around I saw the knives by the stove. I wondered for a brief, yet eternal, moment what it would be like to end it all. I had been praying for rapture, for the second coming of Christ when all the "believers" would be taken up to heaven. This would then be over and my parents would never have to know what I'd gotten myself into. But as I stood there contemplating the knives, I knew in that moment that thoughts are things and words have life. I knew I couldn't play with those thoughts or there would come a time when the thoughts would take over, just like the thoughts of the bankruptcy. They would take on a life of their own. There, standing in that kitchen, I was more afraid of leaving my parents with my mess than I was of dying. And, my supreme fear was what if it is true that suicide separates you from God? I couldn't risk that. Even though I blamed God for some of my misfortune, an eternity without His love was more than I was willing to gamble. In that moment, in the kitchen, I made a choice. I chose to live through my circumstances and begin to fight.

I didn't tell my parents until after I'd left my home a few months later, put my things in storage, and rented a room from an acquaintance. Those were truly the darkest days of my life. My parents were disappointed but not nearly as much as I'd fantasized. Nothing was worse than the machinations of my dreams. I had tortured myself needlessly and relentlessly.

Another thought that plagued me through those difficult years was the question, "Why me?" I was embarrassed and ashamed that I'd left my prominent Naval career, against the advice of so many people, and was now failing for the first time in my life.

I didn't see the plan for why I had to go through what I was enduring. As a matter of fact, I was much like a child having a temper tantrum, only mine was with God. I didn't understand how this could happen to someone He loved. And I knew He loved me. I was sure of it, I thought. Why had He abandoned me? What had I done wrong? I thought He had told me to go down this path, why else would it have been presented to me. How had I missed it? Why me? I cried and pleaded for an answer constantly. If I knew why, maybe I could fix it but it just didn't make sense. Why me?

I remember watching a TV evangelist talking with a woman who had lost her husband and a child and he had asked her if she'd ever asked God the question of "Why me?" She said no. As a follower of Jesus, she realized, "Why not me?" I was crushed. I hadn't lost a loved one, I wasn't physically impaired, I had just lost material things. The holiness of her statement shook me. I asked the "why me" question every day, several times a day. I couldn't understand how God had let this happen to me. I prayed, begged and fell to the floor crying, praying some more. I couldn't get my brain around why I, a beloved child of God, had to go through this stuff.

The question of "why me" plagued me for many, many years. The severity of the embarrassment lessened with time as I worked on myself and improved my circumstances. With the perspective of history, "why me" has changed to "I see." I see now that if I had paid attention to the signs God had showed me, if I had listened to my heart and intuition, if I had taken any other path available to me, I wouldn't have had to go to the depths of despair I went to. But, and that's a huge but, I didn't see, listen, hear, or act on any of the opportunities or signs, that could have prevented the tremendous pain I experienced. I now see that the person who I am today is much stronger, wiser, more compassionate, and more loving than I could have ever been had I not taken the path to here. Yes, it came at a price of a lot of tears, heartache and anguish. My path was a hard fought battle. But I won...eventually.

Your Journey

If it is true that the words you have been saying or thinking have helped create your current reality, take a few moments and observe your words. I use the word "observe", as this is not about blaming yourself. The wonderful thing is that if you recognize the words you've used up until this point, you can now choose new words that can bring you more abundance, joy and hope from this moment forward.

1. So, without condemnation, what are some of the words you've used or thoughts you've had about your situation?

2. Did you have any "ahas" about what you've been thinking or saying about your current circumstances and what appears to be manifesting in your life?

Wherever you are is just fine. It's just where you are. Asking the question "why me" can keep you stuck in the past and unable to move forward. If, up until this point, you have been asking yourself this question, simply notice your feelings for now. Notice that you are in the past and notice your energy level.

3.   What feelings are present?

Bring your thoughts back to the present, to what's in front of you. If you are feeling overwhelmed right now, just breathe. Be kind to yourself, don't use unkind words or call yourself names. You did the best you could, given the information you had at the time. So, be kind. Later, I'll give you more tips on where to place your thoughts. For now, please read on.

LENGTH OF THE JOURNEY

Earlier I stated that I felt that I licked my wounds too long, and that my wish for you in writing this book is a speedier recovery, or an increased momentum from wherever you are now to wherever you want to be. There were choices along the way, things I could have, and would have (in hindsight) done differently. My journey took years and while I wouldn't give up what I've learned, I know in my heart there was a faster way if I had been open to it.

One of the things that led to the length of my journey was that it was so hard for me to accept what had happened. With my bankruptcy and foreclosures, I took on the role of victim. I blamed someone else for what had happened. I also blamed God and myself. The victim role was playing like a record over and over in my mind. I kept searching for clues of what had happened. I reran events over and over again. I was stuck and paralyzed by two questions, "Why me?" and "What if?" What if I'd made a better choice? What if I hadn't gotten out of the Navy? Then there were the shoulds. I should not have done this, I should have done that. Blame and guilt abound in the shoulds and I punished myself far more than anyone else could have punished me.

All those thoughts postponed my acceptance of what was. I needed to simply say this is where I am now without blame or guilt, or the accompanying accusations of "How could you have let this happen?" I knew where I wanted to go, but by refusing to accept and continuing to run those accusing scripts through my mind, I was keeping one foot stuck in the past. I constantly looked over my shoulder, reminding myself of what I had let happen, especially as things started to get better. I would remind myself of my irresponsibility and that I didn't deserve to be happy or prosperous since I squandered what I had. I constantly accused myself of being stupid, a word that wasn't even allowed in my home growing up because of its severe and limiting connotations. All of this served to keep me from moving forward more than an inch at a time.

Acceptance of what happened without blame and condemnation, was important to my recovery. The companion to acceptance is forgiveness. This one was also a tough one to learn. First, I asked God to forgive me for what I'd done, for losing all the money and for those I hurt in the process. I also had to forgive the individual I blamed as the catalyst for my downfall; the woman who brought me into the sales company. I allowed her to persuade me into making a large investment that was not in my best interest. I really struggled with this one since at the time I held her responsible for what had happened.

As I accepted my role, took responsibility for my actions and admitted that no one held a gun to my head or threatened me in any way, I was able to open up to the possibility of forgiving her. Prior to making the investment, my gut instinct told me something was wrong but I did not listen. I was too afraid to ask questions and I trusted others too much. I allowed myself to be in that situation. I could have said no. Oprah Winfrey said that you don't forgive for the other person, you forgive for yourself. The other person probably doesn't even know you're holding a grudge or unforgiveness. That helped me forgive this individual. As long as I held onto unforgiveness and blame, I kept the other person very present in my life and that's not what I wanted.

It didn't happen overnight, but I was able to eventually forgive and let go. To forgive and let go means that I let go of the judgments against them and myself. And, in moving forward, to not let the same thing happen again. One of the key learnings of my Masters of Arts in Spiritual Psychology at the University of Santa Monica, was self-forgiveness; i.e. forgiving myself for any judgments I hold about myself, someone else or an event. This exercise has an amazing freedom to it because we truly do not know why something occurred. It allows me to get to a place of compassion that says, "I forgive myself for judging myself as stupid for filing bankruptcy. I forgive myself for judging myself as a bad person for losing my homes. I forgive myself for judging that woman as a bad person who took advantage of me. I forgive myself for judging myself as weak for not having listened to my intuition. I forgive myself for judging myself as wrong or bad for hurting anyone as a result of my business or my bankruptcy."

I've also effectively used an exercise from the *5 Gifts for an Abundant Life* by Reverend Diane Harmony (I've included it for you in Appendix A). In this exercise, you write a letter to the individual regarding the situation and how you feel/felt about what happened. Then you write a letter back to yourself how you wish they would respond. The letter isn't something you share with the other individual(s). It is purely for you and your heart. You can burn both letters if you choose.

Forgiving others was an important aspect of my moving forward on my journey to abundance. Forgiving God was another. There was a part of me that always knew that God wasn't punishing me for something I did wrong but there was a larger part that thought contrary. Everything in my life seemed to indicate that God had abandoned me, forsaken me. I prayed and prayed for assistance and I saw no visible improvement. In hindsight, there were so many miracles going on around me. I just did not notice. You see I never went hungry, I always had food. There was a brief time without a car, but I lived and worked on a wonderful bus route. I was never truly homeless, although I moved a lot that first year. I gained greater compassion for the homeless than I could have ever had prior to this seemingly disastrous event. I always sent them blessings, and still do, since the line between our two worlds is so thin.

I felt guilty for judging God as failing me. I wrote both of those forgiveness letters in reference to God and reached a true understanding of the grace He's given me.

The hardest one for me to forgive, and the last one, was myself. I felt that if I let myself off the hook I might be capable of doing it again. I had a lot of debt, and not just in credit cards. It was never my intention to default in paying anyone. It was completely out of integrity with who I knew myself to be. For me, filing bankruptcy didn't wipe the slate clean on my heart. I carried the ramifications of embarrassment and guilt with me long after I knew God had forgiven me. What right did I have to succeed if I'd hurt others?

A few years ago, while in one of the "5 GIFTS" workshops, I heard myself picking on my younger self with the "should haves", "why's?" and "that was stupid!" What came to mind was, "Love Her." Just that simple phrase began to shift the energy of what I was feeling about myself during that time. What "Love Her" signified to me was that she (the younger me) did the absolute best she could, given the information she had at the time. If I'd known then what I know now it would not have happened. I know this because I've learned to listen to my intuition and to hear the still small voice of God; two amazing gifts from my journey. As I forgave myself and let go of the shame and guilt I carried every day, I began to move faster on my journey to abundance, able to focus forward without looking back.

Remember, forgiveness has little to do with the other person and everything to do with you and moving forward in your life. For me, unforgiveness held me in the past and prevented me from dusting myself off and moving forward quicker. Forgiveness is one of the greatest gifts I've given myself. But, in letting go of unforgiveness and blaming, I also had to let go of my story. I had to let go of the drama and victim role of losing all of my material things. I had to continue to work on my thoughts and my words. I had to find ways to change my circumstances.

Your Journey

Acceptance and forgiveness are not for the faint of heart.

1. Have you accepted your situation as a matter of fact rather than judgment? Are you willing to? One way to accept where you are is to state objectively, "I am behind in my bills, my rent, mortgage or car payment." What are your feelings about your situation? For example, I'm mad, sad, afraid, embarrassed, hurt, etc. Write them below:

2. Is there someone, even God or yourself, that you blame for getting you into your present situation?

3. Are you open to letting go of your connection to the past?

4. Are you open to forgiving God, yourself or another?

I encourage you now, for your own healing, to go to the exercise in Appendix A. Even if you're not quite ready to do it, go and familiarize yourself with it. When you're done, return here and write down your thoughts and experiences from spending time with this exercise.

Wherever you are is absolutely okay. What someone else did may be so horrific to you that you aren't ready or able (at this time) to forgive them. If that's the case, just be gentle with yourself. Be compassionate with yourself and find ways to love yourself more.

CONFESSIONS OF A SELF-HELP ADDICT

Recently I returned home to find a package at my door. I love getting packages and I was expecting two. As I squinted and bent down to read the label a flutter came to my heart. The return address was Nightingale-Conant. More tapes and CDs for my library. I was elated. Many women buy shoes, I continue to buy self-help books and programs.

In the beautiful apartment that I have now manifested into my life (you'll hear more about that later), I finally have enough space for all of my books. When I unpacked them, I was amazed at just how many I'd collected over the years, most of which were self-help books.

You see, books and tapes became my friends in the months of silence surrounding my bankruptcy. I didn't know how to ask for help but I knew I had to change my thoughts and I couldn't do it alone. I set out on a quest to "fix" myself.

Initially, I was in a bit of a spiritual crisis. At this point, I still blamed God for letting me down. I thought I was following his plan for my life and I had failed miserably. I decided to investigate spiritual teachings to see where I might have missed it. I had been watching Kenneth Copeland, a faith preacher, for many years on his television show, *The Believer's Voice of Victory*. I had been using his biblical teachings since the mid to late 1980's, and even considered him and his wife Gloria, to be my spiritual parents. There were several Bible verses that they preached on that I used to help me understand God's goodness and what God wanted for my life.

I prayed constantly, begging God to make my situation go away. In the beginning I talked at him more than I listened. I had a knowing deep within me that God was a good god and that He cried with me as I cried. I scoured the Bible looking for verses that supported my notion. I read about the plight of Job and his restoration and prayed for my own. I clung to many TV evangelists that spoke a positive message of an abundant God, one who would take care of my needs. By attending faith conventions like Kenneth Copeland's West Coast Believers Convention, I learned that God wanted me to prosper. I spent what money I could on books and tapes that taught me this new way to think and believe. I relied on these verses for direction and hope:

Jeremiah 29:11 – "For I know the plans I have for you," declares the Lord, "plans to prosper you and not to harm you, plans to give you hope and a future."

Matthew 7:7 – "Ask and it will be given to you; seek and you will find; knock and the door will be opened to you. 8For everyone who asks receives; he who seeks finds; and to him who knocks, the door will be opened."

Matthew 19:26 – "...with God all things are possible."

Mark 11:24 – "Therefore I tell you, whatever you ask for in prayer, believe that you have received it, and it will be yours."

Philippians 4: 13, 19 – "I can do everything through him who gives me strength…And my God will meet all your needs according to his glorious riches in Christ Jesus."

Ephesians 3:20 – "Now to him who is able to do immeasurably more than all we ask or imagine, according to his power that is at work within us…"

And my favorite:

John 10:10 – "I have come that they may have life, and that they may have *it* more abundantly." (NKJV) The Amplified Bible states that verse as – "I came that they may have and enjoy life, and have it in abundance (to the full, till it overflows)" (AMP).

Along with my spiritual quest, I also spent hours in bookstores searching for books to help me get out of my situation. One that I discovered is *The Power of Your Subconscious Mind* by Dr. Joseph Murphy (Bantam, 1982). I still pick this book up year after year and continue to find new ways to take my circumstances to the next level. I've purchased at least a dozen copies for friends and coworkers over the years.

Murphy refers to the subconscious as a "miracle-working power." This power can be used for healing illness, gaining wealth and success, improving marriages and other relationships and much more. While my copy of the book is highlighted, underlined, and dog-eared, with numerous multicolored tags throughout the book, the section I used most was "How to Use the Power of Your Subconscious for Wealth."

I started reading this book in 1997, the year after my bankruptcy had been discharged by the court, when I was barely making enough money to cover my bills. Below are the words I clung to in hopes of a better life.

"The Ideal Method for Building a Wealth Consciousness

Perhaps you are saying as you read this chapter, 'I need wealth and success.' This is what you do: Repeat for about five minutes to yourself three or four times a day, 'Wealth. Success.' These words have tremendous power. They represent the inner power of the subconscious mind. Anchor your mind on this substantial power within you; then condition and circumstances corresponding to their nature and quality will be manifested in your life. You are not saying, 'I am wealthy,' you are dwelling on real powers within you. There is no conflict in the mind when you say, 'Wealth.' Furthermore, the feeling of wealth will well up within you as you dwell on the idea of wealth.

The feeling of wealth produces wealth; keep this in mind at all times. Your subconscious mind is like a bank, a sort of universal financial institution. It magnifies whatever you deposit or impress upon it whether it is the idea of wealth or of poverty. Choose wealth."

In later chapters you will see how I applied this and other things that I learned.

Another effort to expand my mind came about the same time with a resolution to take one class a month at the Learning Annex in San Diego. While I did not make it every month, I did attend some fascinating courses.

One such class that caught my eye was *Making a Living Without a Job* by Barbara J. Winter (Bantam, 1993). I found her lecture and book by the same title wonderful as they honored my entrepreneurial spirit and my diverse talents and interests. The book sparks discovery by using exercises to uncover passions, abilities, motivations and dreams. She gives numerous inspirational examples of people who took a hobby and created a successful, lucrative business and lifestyle.

One principle from the book I gravitated to was "Creating Multiple Profit Centers." In this chapter, Winter introduces the idea of developing spin-off businesses around one central theme or business, as well as creating unrelated profit centers. Winter gives the following explanation of profit centers:

"For purposes of illustration, let's use some easy numbers. Suppose you decide that your long-range goal is to create five profit centers each earning $10,000 a year, and you want to accomplish that within the next five years. You have two ideas that you can get started with and another that needs more thought, and you aren't certain what the additional two will be. You think your first two schemes could be started simultaneously.

You've isolated your first step: create two $10,000-a-year income sources. Breaking that down, you'll discover that your monthly goal for each will be just over $800, making the weekly target $200. Psychologically, earning $200 is feasible — even if the larger amount seems difficult. Knowing what your financial goal is makes it easier to determine what action you'll need to take to accomplish it."

So I decided to look for ways to add profit centers. I also used a strategy from Phil Laut's book *Money is my Friend*, which says that you should make your first $100 from any enterprise before deciding if you want to continue with it.

Throughout this period I continued to read everything I could get my hands on to improve my situation. In addition to using the mantra "Wealth," I used visualization techniques from Dr. Wayne Dyers book, *You'll See it When You Believe it* and meditations from his tape series "Manifest Your Destiny." I stepped up my quest to know God more fully by reading the *Bible, A Course in Miracles* and Marianne Williamson's discussions of *A Course*, as well as reading her other books.

There were also numerous books I read that were recommended by various distributorship organizations I was affiliated with at the time. *The Magic of Thinking Big*, by David J. Schwartz, Ph.D., and the *Magic of Believing*, by Claude M. Bristol, were just two that helped me connect with believing and dreaming beyond my current circumstances. These books and others are listed in the resource section, and are wonderful aids to choose new life goals, create a plan and stay focused as you move forward on your journey.

I also began reading more and more about prosperity. Somewhere in my journey I learned about Catherine Ponder. The only book dog-eared more than *The Power of Your Subconscious Mind,* is her book *The Dynamic Laws of Prosperity* (DeVorss & Company, 1985). Both books were written in the early 1960s, and opened my mind to God's desire for me to prosper. The Bible verse "I have come that they may have life, and that they may have *it* more abundantly " (NKJV) took a greater meaning as I read these books. In *The Dynamic Laws of Prosperity*, Ponder gives numerous affirmations to attract wealth as well as be prosperous in all areas of ones life.

I printed many affirmations on 3x5 cards and business cards to carry with me at all times. A few of my favorites are:

- "EVERYTHING AND EVERYBODY PROSPERS ME NOW."
- "I GIVE THANKS THAT EVERY DAY IN EVERY WAY I AM GROWING RICHER AND RICHER."
- "I EXPECT LAVISH ABUNDANCE EVERY DAY IN EVERY WAY IN MY LIFE AND AFFAIRS. I SPECIFICALLY EXPECT AND GIVE THANKS FOR LAVISH ABUNDANCE TODAY!"

I used this passage many, many times to help me move forward in my prosperity:

"...beginning right now, whenever you think about money, whether it be income, outgo, the amount in your savings or investments — begin mentally increasing your supply by thinking of ten times that amount coming to you. This is a delightful and fascinating technique for increasing your money.

For instance, look in your wallet. Suppose there is $5 there. Look at it and declare: 'I GIVE THANKS THAT THIS $5 IS BUT A SYMBOL OF THE INEXHAUSTIBLE SUBSTANCE OF THE UNIVERSE. I GIVE THANKS THAT TEN TIMES THIS MUCH OR $50 IS NOW ON ITS WAY TO ME AND QUICKLY MANIFESTS IN PERFECT WAYS.' ...By multiplying everything by ten, your thinking automatically shifts from lack to prosperity. Since the mind quickly responds to *definite figures*, it will seem as though heaven and earth are working to propel money in your direction."

So from all that I've shared with you, you can see that there is a wealth of knowledge that I found that has made an impact in my life. In more recent years I've used "Get the Edge" by Tony Robbins, *Building Your Field of Dreams* by Mary Manin Morrissey, *Your Best Life Now* by Joel Osteen, numerous books by Jack Canfield including *The Success Principles*, *The Power of Intention* by Wayne Dyer, *Ask and It Shall Be Given* and *Law of Attraction* by Esther and Jerry Hicks, and *The Secret* by Rhonda Byrne, and many, many more. Being so fractioned in my efforts could be one reason for the length of my journey. I grasped at anything I could find, never really focusing longer than a few weeks or months, except for the "wealth" mantra, which I've continued throughout the years. However, I must say that on this side of abundance, I am grateful for all of it and still use much of my learning from those early years today as I continue to prosper and to teach others. No matter whether you focus on one program, book or teaching and attain overnight success or, like me, meander through the woods a bit, your journey will be perfect. You simply have to choose to look for assistance that resonates with you.

Your Journey

I've mentioned in this chapter several books and tapes that you can use for your journey. I've included in Appendix B numerous other resources that I've used along the way. Before you go out and purchase them, however, my recommendation is to first check them out of the library. Also, most, if not all, libraries have their own bookstore where they sell used books for as little as $.50. I've built much of my self-help collection this way, which has saved me a lot of money. As I was coming out of debt, I also asked for gift certificates to bookstores for birthdays and Christmas. That provided me with hours of fun research at the bookstore that furthered me on my journey.

1. Choose at least one affirmation or verse that reso-
    nated with you the most from this chapter:

2. If that affirmation is too large a stretch for you to
    really believe, reword it here so that it is a smaller
    leap of faith. For example, if "I give thanks that every
    day in every way I am growing richer and richer"

feels unrealistic right now, try, "I give thanks that every day in every way riches are making their way to me":

3. Write out your affirmation on a 3x5 card or print out on the computer. Place it in several locations in your home. I have mine on the wall across from my bed so I see it every morning and night. I also have one on my bathroom mirror (I move it to the inside of my medicine cabinet before guests arrive) and sometimes I'll have one at my front door so I have a reminder just as I'm leaving for the day.

4. What type of learning resonates with you best? Are you more visual, auditory or kinesthetic? Do you prefer Books – DVD – Lectures? Really take time here to think about how you learn best and choose avenues that will support that.

I encourage you to start using the "wealth" mantra exercise mentioned in this chapter. What would it feel like to have enough? What can you believe for right now? Start with whatever is present for you at this point. We will revisit this exercise throughout the book. Just be willing to start activating the feeling of wealth within you today.

DO OVER

In mid-1996, with the bankruptcy officially discharged and my resignation from the sales company complete, it was time to try to recover from the mess I felt I'd made. I missed the military and I wondered if they would take me back after a bankruptcy. I decided to try. I did my due diligence to return, getting endorsements and speaking with many people, however it proved to be a bit of a struggle. I pondered the proverbial question - can you ever really go back? Then, I considered the reasons I got out of the Navy and decided to discontinue my pursuit and to look at my life as a do over.

During my financial troubles, I gained quite a bit of weight. The woman I was staying with, a friend of a friend, recommended a doctor who she had gone to for weight loss. So off I went. I had to weigh in each week and was seeing progress. I'd worked for a doctor many years earlier and offered my services to the doctor's wife, his office manager. She took me up on it and I began working just a few hours a week around the office answering phones and scheduling appointments. The doctor was a psychiatrist (MD). I had wanted to study psychology many years before and this gave me the opportunity to evaluate the field. Plus, the doctor and his wife were wonderful people, and so I really enjoyed working at the office. You might think I had an excellent opportunity to get free counseling while I worked for the doctor. Unfortunately, I didn't take advantage of that. I told them only a little about what I'd been through and lived quietly with my shame and guilt.

Within six months of working for the doctor, *The Power of Your Subconscious Mind* found it's way to me. I started working with the wealth and success ideas I mentioned in the previous chapter. First thing in the morning and last thing at night, as well as several times throughout the day, I said the word "wealth" over and over again to myself. The more I used the mantra, the more abundance came to me. I wasn't making a lot of money at the doctor's office but they were far more generous than I could have expected. I began thinking about what it would feel like if all of my bills were paid on time and my needs were met. Then once I attained that, I moved to what it would feel like to have an extra $50 in the bank. You may be asking why not ask for more? At the time, that's all I could believe was possible. From there I progressed incrementally to what it would feel like to have $100, $500, $1000, and upwards of $15,000 or more in savings. It took years, but I have attained it. When I used the mantra coupled with the feelings I got as I visualized, I manifested promotions, raises and even possessions.

I still use the "wealth" mantra today, repeating the word "wealth" to myself first thing in the morning, last thing at night, and throughout the day, as I look to attract more into my life. Living an abundant life is not only about having more money. For me, it includes an abundance of health, wonderful relationships and experiences, as well as opportunities. I am so grateful for this simple yet powerful technique and its lasting impact.

When I discovered *Making a Living* I was still working as an office manager and also helping with the doctor's website. I began looking at those as two separate profit centers. I wasn't making the kind of money I had been making in the military but I liked what I was doing. I decided to look for ways to add profit centers. I also used Phil Laut's strategy to make my first $100 from any enterprise before deciding if I wanted to continue.

The next profit center I added was quite unique and contradictory to where I was at the time. I managed bill payments for wealthy people. I was introduced to three separate people who had significant wealth but needed assistance getting their bills paid. I realized that no matter how much or little someone has, bills are no fun. And, the only real difference was a few extra zeros. Each client handled their money completely differently, which gave me insight into new money management techniques, some of which I still use today. For instance, I saw that they all paid their credit card balances in full each month, whether it was $100 or $10,000. They also used credit cards with mileage rewards in order to gain free travel. It took me several years to qualify for a mileage card and to solidify the practice of paying my balance in full each month. But I put in the time and am now enjoying some of the benefits of the wealthy.

My wealthy clients lived in the most beautiful, affluent areas in and around San Diego, California. One day, I drove around La Jolla, one of the most prosperous communities in America, looking at the lovely homes and luxury cars. I pondered that if God exists and made all of these beautiful things, why couldn't I enjoy them, too? By this time I'd forgiven God and I knew He'd forgiven me. I knew He loved me and if he did, wouldn't he want me to have nice things? Why should they be reserved for other people?

I went to a nearby lake a few days later and contemplated the concept of abundance in nature. I looked at the grass and the leaves on the trees and thought of Matthew 6:25-30:

> 25"Therefore I tell you, do not worry about your life, what you will eat or drink; or about your body, what you will wear. Is not life more important than food, and the body more important than clothes? 26Look at the birds of the air; they do not sow or reap or store away in barns, and yet your heavenly Father feeds them. Are you not much more valuable than they? 27Who of you by worrying can add a single hour to his life?
>
> 28And why do you worry about clothes? See how the lilies of the field grow. They do not labor or spin. 29Yet I tell you that not even Solomon in all his splendor was dressed like one of these. 30If that is how God clothes the grass of the field, which is here today and tomorrow is thrown into the fire, will he not much more clothe you, O you of little faith?"

Being exposed to wealth from the inside helped me dream bigger and open my mind to other potential profit centers. Two clients I worked with used computerized systems but the other wouldn't, and I had to write those checks by hand. This was not efficient for me, a self-professed computer geek. But when I mentioned switching to a computerized program, I sensed some trepidation. Even the clients who let me use a system were hesitant to learn how to use it themselves. All of my clients were baby boomers or older and when I looked at their hesitancy to learn computers, I got an idea. I decided to develop a computer program to help people new to computers. It would teach basic computer skills like word processing, email and saving and finding documents.

Using my mother as the model of my target market, since she frequently called me with computer questions, in April 1998 I developed "Quick Computing for Women." I sold a couple of my computer programs but soon discovered I had an uphill battle. I realized the people I had written the program for just wanted me to do the task for them rather than learn how to do it themselves. Remember, this was 1998 and the Internet was new. One of my hopes in creating the program was to duplicate myself and thereby make more money but it just didn't seem like it was working out that way. I knew I couldn't make enough money personally instructing everyone. So, using Laut's $100 test, I decided that "Quick Computing" might not be my ticket to fame and fortune.

Still, I loved computers, programming and especially the Internet. I knew that I wanted to work in that field. In early 1999, the doctor I worked for retired. I still ran his website that was making a little money. One day a friend of his offered me an opportunity doing Internet research. My job was to research whether a patent existed on a particular technology that he had submitted a patent on. The patent process takes approximately eighteen months to be reviewed and his was due for review soon. I was getting paid well for this job and was quite happy about that. The job, however, was lonely and tedious. I spent eight hours a day looking for a needle in a haystack. While I was enjoying getting paid substantially more than I'd made working for the doctor, the potential of being part of the new dotcom world was enticing, and I couldn't stop thinking about it. Internet millionaires seemed to be born every minute. Then one day, six weeks after I began my project, I found what I had been looking for. I discovered that a patent did exist almost identical to his. I knew my job was over that day and it was.

I wasn't sure what God had in store for me next when this position ended. I started to get a bit nervous but God's timing was, of course, perfect. My parents called just after that job ended and asked if I could meet their moving truck in a nearby state the following Saturday, since they would not arrive from the east coast until that night. I drove over and was able to stay almost a week with them, which was wonderful. I was talking to God quite a bit that week. When I arrived back, I saw an advertisement for an upcoming local technical job fair at a company I had admired for years. I had even applied for a job with them eight months earlier, with no luck. I prayed hard before leaving for the fair, armed with numerous resumes. Most of the Internet jobs available were for high-end programmers, with skills I hadn't kept up since I had received my Masters in Information Systems when I was still in the Navy in 1992. However, I knew one web coding skill very well, HTML (hypertext-markup language), and this company had a position called HTML Specialist. Thank you, God. I got hired a few weeks later and have been working for them ever since. As an entry-level position, the pay wasn't the big money of the dotcom boom. I also didn't know to ask for options and wasn't offered any.

You may be thinking that I sold out by taking a corporate job, leaving my entrepreneurial interests behind. But, I was given a chance to do something I loved, which was code web pages, and it was more money than I had made since I left the service. As my corporate career demanded so much attention and time (well over fifty hours a week, sometimes closer to seventy), I let go of my other profit centers. I did hold on to my intention of making an additional $10,000 a year and each year it has worked out that I've continued to average that gain.

When one area of a person's life is falling apart, like with significant debt or a bankruptcy, there are generally other areas that are in peril as well. That was definitely my experience. By 2000, I found myself recovering from my debt, but nowhere near where I wanted to be. I purchased the tape series "Get the Edge" by Tony Robbins, when I saw him on QVC in 2000. I'd admired Tony for years and had previously purchased some of his other books and tapes.

I had just been hired at the company and was ready to take my life to the next level. My self-esteem still needed work but my dreams were big.

On the tapes, Tony asks the listener to take a close, honest look at our lives and identify three areas that were disgusting to us. My three were 1) I owed back taxes and felt haunted by it, 2) I had gained significant weight while I was broke and 3) I was in a relationship with a man and I knew I needed to end it but didn't know how. I listened to the entire tape series one time and then replayed the tape on getting results. A year and a half later I saw Tony again on QVC and realized that all of my back taxes had been paid, I'd lost forty pounds and I was out of the relationship. I had not been consciously working "Get the Edge," but it definitely had an impact on how I thought about myself and what I wanted for my life. I was quite impressed with the program and with myself.

I continued to take classes over the years at the Learning Annex. In March 2003, I took a class called "Effortless Prosperity," taught by a man named Bijan Anjomi. That night I had one of the most important "aha" moments of my life. He said that we have two voices inside of us – one is our higher power, God or Spirit and the other is our ego. The voice of our higher power always brings us peace while the other always brings us turmoil. I sat there in stunned silence flashing back on my "why me" episodes years before. I'd thought I'd heard from God when I made the critical decision to join the sales organization; a decision that so drastically altered my financial course. But thinking back, I specifically remember being out of peace and in great angst. In that moment I realized it hadn't been God's fault at all. I just didn't know that it wasn't Him. I knew that I was in turmoil but used my head and not my better judgment, my intuition, to make my decision. In that knowing, I found peace and more forgiveness for God, the person who signed me up, and even for myself. Oprah Winfrey frequently quotes Maya Angelou, "when you know better, you do better." With this new knowing, I knew that my life would be different going forward. Oprah also said, "Doubt means don't." I do wish I'd learned that back in 1993.

I trust my intuition more today because of the journey I've been on. I learned many lessons on this journey about wealth, my talents and abilities, my determination and about staying in peace. I am grateful I saw my life as a do over, an opportunity to change my circumstances and my life.

Your Journey

1. If you could improve any three areas of your life (e.g. finances, weight, home, career, relationships, spirituality, health) over the next year, which improvements would make your heart sing?

2. Now prioritize those three. Which area is the most important, urgent or pressing for you at this time? Reorder your priorities here:

3. Are there any action steps that you immediately think of as you review your prioritized list? Capture them here. Don't worry. No actions are required at this time. You will have an opportunity to commit to your next steps later but right now just write them down.

One of the challenges I had as I began taking steps to improve my situation was continuing to be gentle and kind with myself when I thought of what got me into the situation. Are you being judgmental and critical of yourself for being in this situation? As you begin to see your life as a do over, try an exercise I used to encourage myself to move forward:

If a close friend came to you wanting to improve one or all three of the above problems, what might you tell him/her? Is that the same way you're thinking about your own situation? Can you be as loving, kind and forgiving with yourself as you would be with them?

4. Write yourself a sweet note of encouragement now:

Being kind to yourself may be new for you, but I encourage you to start where you are. You are a good person and you deserve a new friend - you.

TAPPING INTO THE BLESSINGS

tithe - "To contribute or pay a tenth part of (one's annual income)."

I know that tithing can make people cringe and conjure up images of evangelists and preachers begging for money. I felt the same way for many years. In fact, I resented God for quite sometime when I had barely enough money and yet I felt I had to tithe. However, I can truly say that I tithed my way out of debt.

During the dark, lonely days after I filed bankruptcy, I still had a little money coming in from my sales and commissions. I continued to go to church seeking answers to what had gone wrong in my life. I truly thought that God had led me to the decision to be a sales rep, and I just couldn't understand why he deserted me. It made no sense. I really thought I was doing His work and yet I had failed so miserably. I knew He loved me and yet here I was a failure, depressed, embarrassed, broke and losing everything I owned. And yet I still put money in the offering plate at church as it passed me. It may not have been the full 10% but I gave what I felt I could. I felt guilty if I didn't.

As I gave, within myself I would say "Here God, I don't have enough, but take it." Now, that statement could be interpreted more than one way. It could mean, "God, I love you so much and while I don't have enough, I trust that you are with me and that you are providing a way for me." But how I meant it was, "God, you have taken everything else from me, why not take my tithe. I've given you everything and you have forsaken me. Take my crumbs, too."

Much like a defiant teenager, I shoved what little I had towards God. My heart was not right. It soon became clear to me that God didn't want or need my money that way and it also became clear that I was to stop tithing. And I felt like I was given strict instructions not to tithe until my heart was right. The bible passage I was reminded of is 2 Corinthians 9:6-8:

"[6]Remember this: Whoever sows sparingly will also reap sparingly, and whoever sows generously will also reap generously. [7]Each man should give what he has decided in his heart to give, not reluctantly or under compulsion, for God loves a cheerful giver. [8]And God is able to make all grace abound to you, so that in all things at all times, having all that you need, you will abound in every good work."

For several months, I tithed my time, and not money, working at a church in their toddler care program. As the time wore on, I really wanted to tithe off my income again, more out of embarrassment that as the basket passed me during the offering than for correct motives. I began reading Malachi 3:10 over and over again, "'Bring the whole tithe into the storehouse, that there may be food in my house. Test me in this,' says the

LORD Almighty, 'and see if I will not throw open the floodgates of heaven and pour out so much blessing that you will not have room enough for it.'"

I devoured books by Catherine Ponder and others on prosperity and tithing and my heart began to change. I really wanted to pay homage to God for the gifts He'd given me, including food, friends and income (however small). Each dollar I earned felt like a personal gift from God. I wanted to give my first fruits and thank Him. For weeks, I asked God if I could tithe and the answer was in my spirit no. Suddenly, out of great humility, thankfulness, and love for God, one Sunday when I asked the answer was yes and I was so grateful.

I began tithing off any income that came in. I wasn't making that much, just working several odd jobs. This was a few months before I started working for the doctor. I began with a check of $50 from my sales and by sending a tithe of $5 to a television ministry. I wanted to prove myself trustworthy to God. Matthew 25:23 states, "Well done, good and faithful servant! You have been faithful with a few things; I will put you in charge of many things." I understood during my tithing hiatus that for God to bless me with more I had to prove myself to Him that I would not squander his money and I wanted to be trusted with much more. I sent checks of $5 or $7 several times a month as the money came in.

You might be wondering if I slipped. Of course I did. What I discovered, though, was that on the months I didn't pay my tithe first, I ran out of money before the end of the month. However, in months I tithed first, I always had enough. Maybe just barely, but it was enough. Also, as I mentioned, I never went hungry, someone always shared a meal with me or gave me something, including clothes and furniture. I was making ends meet and that's all that mattered at the time. I just wanted to get some breathing room from all my debt.

Soon I was giving $10, $30, $50 checks of tithes. I began taking tithing classes and learned even more about tithing and the blessings from it. A common question is whether you tithe off the gross or net of your income. In one series called the "4Ts, Tithing of Your Time, Talents and Treasures" by Stretton Smith and taught by my good friend, Reverend Diane Harmony, I learned to tithe off the gross, before taxes are taken out. That truly puts God first in your life. I've also heard the response, "Do you want your blessings off the net or the gross?" Tithing off the gross was a leap of faith for me and took some getting used to.

A couple of years after I had settled my issues with tithing, I was given a $10,000 bonus from work as a part of a program to keep employees during the dot-com days. My after-tax portion of that bonus totaled just over $5,400. How much do you think I would have tithed if I hadn't settled this with God? Since I was committed to tithing, I lovingly wrote the check for $1,000 thanking God for what he'd given me as I truly had been blessed. I was truly grateful since I had $4,400 more than I had the day before. That has occurred more than once under other circumstances and as I continue to prove myself trustworthy, He continues to bless me with more.

When my paycheck is deposited every two weeks, I honor God with my tithes and thank him for what he's blessed me with. That's before I pay rent, buy groceries, or spend anything on myself. For years I've also used an affirmation I modified from *The Dynamic Laws of Prosperity* to remind me of the blessings of tithing. I hold my tithe check in my hands and say "God, I am giving $400 thereby invoking the laws of receiving. I expect 100 times this amount ($40,000) to manifest now to meet every demand." Now, that may raise issues of "giving to get." But in another version of Malachi 3:10, God says to "…prove Me now by it…if I will not open the windows of heaven for you and pour you out a blessing…" (AMP) I use the affirmation to align myself with the vibration of abundance and as a reminder of my "laying up treasures in heaven" and that by putting God first in my life, I can expect to be blessed. I have never received a check back for the amount named in the affirmation but I've also not wanted for anything since I settled the issue of tithing. My income has more than doubled in five years. I live debt free, except for my car payment, which I can now pay in full if I choose. With each car payment or apartment increase, I've received a raise almost to the penny of the increase. And it did not always coincide with an annual work review. God planned it. Not me, and not my employer.

I would be lying if I told you I was not tempted to use that money in other ways. I could drive a nicer car and live in a house instead of an apartment. The truth is, I have to remind myself of His blessings and that He has taken care of me up until this point He will continue. I give and God provides. I have more to prove that I'm trustworthy to get where I want to go. It started with being trustworthy with $50 and has grown from there. It's been over a decade since God taught me the lesson of getting my heart right, and I've gone from tithing $5 to regularly tithing $400 or more.

Another consideration is where to tithe. I don't currently have a church home so I give where I am fed, where I felt a message or where a spiritual teacher has moved me further on my path towards God. I have also tithed to "Oprah's Angel Network" (www.oprahsangelnetwork.org) because I know that the money is going to help others. There are numerous other organizations you can give to including www.trickleup.org, www.heifer.org, ww.kiva.org to name just a few. Look for organizations that move you and resonate with who you are and what you believe in.

I do look for organizations that also tithe of the tithes they received. Several evangelists I have listened to talked about the benefits of the twice sown seed. To be honest, I want to be twice blessed. As I am a blessing to someone, I do want to be blessed. I want to know that an organization that I give to also give to others. That is important to me, in order to keep abundance flowing for all.

When I began to put God first in my finances and in my life and with the right heart, blessings began to overtake me. I am more grateful every day that He is my Source and my provider.

Your Journey

Tithing is a very personal choice. I've shared with you the difference it made in my life. If you are not currently tithing, write down any resistance that came up during this chapter.

1. What are your thoughts on giving at this time in your life?

2. If you can't tithe money just yet, is there an organization where you can tithe your talents and share your gifts to initiate giving and receiving in your life?

Also, giving any offering with a heart of thanks and gratitude will open your heart and allow more to flow to you. So give a silent blessing to everyone you see tomorrow. If you see someone stuck on the side of the road and you can't stop or help, simply saying, "Send them help" will activate a blessing. You may never know exactly how that blessing helped, but just know it did.

3. In what ways could you be a blessing to someone else tomorrow? Write it down so you activate the action within you. It could be sending silent blessings, calling a friend or writing a thank you note. What are you willing to do?

I encourage you to open up to the possibilities of giving and receiving, sowing and reaping. If it is difficult for you, start with sending silent blessings to everyone you meet. It can take some time to get the giving and receiving cycle moving, but once it does, blessings will find you and begin to overtake you.

———●✦✕✦●———

DREAM BIG

Because of the loss of my homes, I have decided to wait before purchasing another. For me, abundance is also about peace. In September 2001, I was in escrow for a 947-square foot condo in San Diego selling for $220,000. My thought was that was just too much to pay for such a little place. Since my FICO score (a credit score used by lenders to determine how likely a credit user is to pay their bills) was still low and I had only a few thousand in savings, the mortgage on that tiny place started getting higher and higher as the mortgage broker looked for creative financing. I would have to take out personal loans with friends and family, which added to that mortgage. I began to panic and got a sense that I would barely be able to make the nearly $2,000 mortgage, including personal loan payments, and that I would have to either eat at friends homes or be back where I was five years earlier. I finally called my realtor and told her to get me out of the deal, which she did.

I missed out on the big housing boom in San Diego. That condo is now worth well over $500,000, but I have peace, and that for me is worth more than gold. Do I want to own a house again? Sure, when I can truly own it. When I know that I can effortlessly afford it. That is what I've learned from my past.

The company I work for relocated in 2004 and I was able to manifest a lovely apartment in an affluent area that I could afford with ease and grace. I did that by creating and revising a list of what I wanted in my ideal apartment and with lots of prayer that God would lead me to the perfect home. I originally thought I wanted to rent a two-bedroom house large enough for my friends to stay over on weekends, but realized I didn't want the upkeep of a large place. I wanted it to be close to my work and comfortable. I wrote the list repeatedly until I felt I captured my ideal, heartfelt scenario of what I truly wanted.

Here is my final list:
- ✓ Comfortable
- ✓ Everything has a home
- ✓ Open, spacious
- ✓ I can see the TV when standing at the kitchen sink
- ✓ Floor plan is well laid out
- ✓ Office area
- ✓ Places for books/bookcases
- ✓ Lots of cabinets and counter space in kitchen
- ✓ At least 1 ½ bath
- ✓ Walking distance to movie theater, bookstore, coffee shop, library, restaurants
- ✓ Air conditioning, garage and an in-home washer and dryer
- ✓ Large master bedroom with sitting area by the window
- ✓ Single level

- ✓ Private patio/balcony
- ✓ View of mountains, ocean or golf course
- ✓ Easy to maintain
- ✓ Quiet, retreat-like neighborhood
- ✓ Lots of storage, closets and ledges
- ✓ Feels great
- ✓ Within ten miles of work, with highway access
- ✓ Safe and prosperous area
- ✓ Easily affordable with ease and grace

I also knew what God-centered qualities I was looking to create with this list and my new home; security, luxury, abundance, proximity, joy, warmth, serenity, privacy and openness.

I secured temporary housing but still met with a relocation specialist provided by my company. After looking through the sheets of apartments she'd picked out for me based upon my specifications, I selected four for us to visit. I asked her if there were any in my rejection pile that I should reconsider. She said, "Yes, one." I had rejected it because it didn't have a private garage. She explained that it had a parking structure for renters to park on the same level as their apartment that provided a cover to and from their residence. Further, she said that the management was excellent, as was the property. I agreed to look at it and we drove there first. The property was great and I liked the floor plans. However, the kitchen sink didn't quite face the television in the living room on the models that were in my price range. That was a quirky thing I'd wanted for years.

The complex did have many other amenities that were great: the property was gated, it was very retreat-like and quiet, and the management team seemed very helpful and quite nice. I decided to reserve one, just in case. There were people coming in and out of the office leasing available apartments and I wanted to ensure that I got the floor plan I wanted. They would hold the unit for 72 hours, which would give me time to see the other places on my list. Plus, I figured I had my temporary housing to fall back on.

The leasing agent said he had a corner unit that faced a wall where no one could see into the unit. For most people, that was undesirable, and made the unit lower priced than it's counterparts. But for me, that met my privacy need and I said I'd take it and filled out my paperwork. I gave him a brief overview of my financial history just in case something came up on the credit check. I was relieved that nothing came up and that I would no longer have to explain the bankruptcy situation in my past. Now approved, I asked if he could show me the unit. When I walked in, I gasped. The floor plan was open and the kitchen sink faced the living room area and TV. Both the leasing agent and relocation specialist rattled off establishments in the area. I'd seen a multi-plex movie theater when we drove in. They added that a major bookstore and several clothing stores were also within walking distance, as well as a library. I was delighted. Suddenly, I recognized the area and asked if a Costco was nearby as well. When they said yes, I literally squealed with delight. I had landed in a place I had admired from the toll road on my 2-hour treks to school. I'd driven by this area once a month over the course of a year and thought it would be lovely to live there. I didn't have to look at any other places; I was sold.

I absolutely love my home, and all of the items and qualities from my list are there, except for the private garage and the extra bathroom. I really don't have enough visitors to justify the extra bathroom, and I'm certainly happy to have less to clean. And not having a garage turned out to be another gift from God. I gave away or donated thousands of dollars worth of items from my old garages, which freed up so much energy that had me stuck in the past. And I got what I really wanted, a safe, covered place to store my car. Each day as I drive away from it, I look out to a breathtaking view of mountains and thank God for leading me to this exquisite place.

I do look forward to the day when I own a place again. But for now I am enjoying living in a home that meets my needs and wants. And I feel truly abundant.

I continue to manifest amazing results including relationships, improved health and wellness, and wonderful experiences. My Masters of Arts in Spiritual Psychology degree in 2005 was a conscious manifestation and realization of a twenty year dream of mine. I no longer have to prove anything to myself. And, I have many more big dreams, including material possessions. I also want to travel more and have time and money to spend with friends and family. I want to help others to avoid what I went through and most of all, I want to enjoy life and live in peace and harmony.

Your Journey

If you are in significant debt right now it may be difficult to dream beyond just making ends meet. I encourage you to try. Like repeating "wealth" over and over again to yourself with feeling, dreaming can help attract abundance to you. And you can rewrite your dreams any time. You're not locked in.

The "yeah buts" may emerge here. Be playful and non-threatening with yourself as you go through these questions. Be willing to dream, to play and to believe. Most of all, have fun.

1. If you could live anywhere, where would that be? What are the qualities you think living there might bring you? How would that feel?

2. What type of home would you like? How would it feel to have it?

3. What type of car? How would it feel to have it?

4. Where would you like to travel? How would it feel to be there?

5. What types of relationships would you like to have? How would it feel to have them?

6. What would you do if all your bills were paid, your immediate needs were met and you were given $1,000 a day for a full year? How would you feel?

One great way to assist in this process is to create a Dream Board. Cut out pictures of the items on your list and words that inspire or represent what you want in your life. Put them on a poster board or a memory board, in a book or folder or wherever your creativity would like to display what you would like to manifest in your life. Make sure to revisit your Dream Board regularly, to attract what you wish to experience in your life. Again, have fun and give yourself permission to dream!

GRATITUDE AND CONTENTMENT

I have experienced a tremendous number of blessings since my financial challenges in 1995-1996. Some were downright miracles. I'll share a few with you now to honor the angels, both spiritual and human, that I met along my journey.

In the summer of 1996, I attended the Kenneth Copeland Ministries West Coast Believer's (now named "Prosperity") Convention in Anaheim, California. It was July and I had very little money. I was staying with a friend who offered me some food but out of modesty I took just an apple and a cup of soup. At lunch, I went outside to eat my apple. I was quite hungry but I didn't want to spend what little I had on food. I was talking to God the whole way and asking for a sign that everything was going to be okay. I sat on the grass in front of the convention center. A woman and her son sitting nearby called to me and offered me a sandwich. I accepted and joined them. I was immensely grateful and thanked them for their generosity to a stranger.

Another amazing miracle occurred when an old car I was driving broke down on a busy highway towards the end of the evening rush hour. I didn't have a cellular phone and I was in between two off-ramps where there was no emergency call box. I was so scared sitting there, praying for a miracle. After about ten minutes, I got out of my car and started to walk up the ramp to a nearby gas station. It was dark with no street lamps, and because I'm black and was wearing dark clothes, I was quite worried that drivers wouldn't see me as they came around the corner. After I'd walked a third of the way up the ramp, an SUV pulled over. The driver turned on the interior light so I could see she was a woman. This highway angel told me she stopped because someone had done that for her once. She dropped me off at the gas station and I contacted AAA. On a dark night, this lovely Caucasian woman was moved to stop for me, a stranded African-American woman. It really was a miracle to me and the answer to my prayer. I still pray for her today and send blessings to her and her family.

Another big blessing has been watching my credit rating improve. When my car died, it had only been 3 ½ years since the discharge of my bankruptcy. A used auto dealer was willing to give me a loan, but with a whopping 21.9% interest! I needed a car to get to work, so. I signed the papers. I went on the Internet as soon as I got home, and I was approved the next day for a 13.99% loan. It was still high, but much better. When I wanted to trade my car in for a newer one a couple of years later, I opened an account at a local credit union, because I'd heard it might be easier to get a loan through a credit union. A woman from the bank sat down with me and ran my credit report for my Visa ® ATM card. I told her my history. She was so kind and gentle with me as she went over my credit history. She wisely told me to give it another six months of good behavior with my credit and then apply for a loan. I did and six months later I had tears in my eyes as I was approved for a 5.99% loan. I uttered, "But that's a regular person's rate." It was June 2002, and my credit rating had been restored.

A month prior to opening my credit union account, I started looking at different types of cars. I continued to look while I was waiting to apply for the loan. While I loved and appreciated my Toyota Corolla, I was moving up in the company and I wanted something that reflected my growing wealth consciousness. I decided on a BMW or Mercedes Benz. The best I could do at first was drive by the dealership and wish I had the courage to go in. Then I began focusing my "wealth" mantra on my new car. In the mornings and before drifting off to sleep at night, I would feel what it would be like to open my garage door and see a luxury car that I could effortlessly afford. I'd also feel what it might be like to drive it. The more I worked on the feeling the more courage I got to go actually look at one. The BMW dealership was next to a Toyota dealership, so I parked my car there and walked over to look at the BMWs. I was trading up out of my comfort zone so that was the best I could do. I also thought they wouldn't take me seriously if they saw my car. I did this several times over the course of a month, not ready to commit to a test-drive, while continuing to practice my "wealth" mantra. Finally, I went to test drive a Mercedes and loved the car. I went on the Internet and researched the area dealers and prices.

This whole process took about eight months and what I began to realize was that my old car was just fine.

It would be nice to have a luxury car but I didn't "need" one. I didn't even need a new car, for that matter. One Friday on the way to see a very close friend, who'd been with me through the lean years, I realized how grateful I was for all that I'd been through. I had a good car that ran well, I lived in the wonderful city of San Diego, and I had my health, family and friends. I thanked God for all of it and in that moment I felt pure contentment. The next day, I decided to go out test-driving one more time. I had a hidden motive; one of the dealerships was giving away free movie tickets. But I figured, why not look at a few more cars? Before I left, I took ten minutes to pray that the day would be successful. I went to four dealerships and was tempted by a previously owned BMW. It had over 45,000 miles, so I decided to sleep on it.

I quickly stopped by the nearby Mercedes dealership, my last planned stop. It was 5 PM and I thought they were closed. I spotted a tan (Desert Silver) C230 and looked at the price. It was $5,000 less than a similar car at another dealership and this one only had just over 18,000 miles. A salesman came over, took me for a test drive and I was sold. He also said it was discounted an additional $1000, even though they said previously they wouldn't do that. Since it was a Saturday night, he had to run a credit check even though I had secured my own funding. I explained what might come up on the report, saying that I had a failed business that resulted in a bankruptcy. I was looking down at my lap when he said, "your credit is fine, and we would have given you a loan." I looked at him, puzzled. He said I had a 724 FICO score. I asked him to say that again and he showed me his computer screen.

I was shocked and elated that day. Driving off the lot having just traded in my Toyota Corolla for a Mercedes Benz, I had the amazing feeling that I'd finally arrived. A few months prior, I had received a platinum credit card and experienced the same emotion. In only six years, the hard work and modest gains I'd made to improve both my income and credit rating had paid off. I'd proven to myself and to credit companies that I was once again a responsible member of society. And, in both instances, I got on my knees that evening to thank God. I wasn't thanking him for the actual things. He'd brought me through my wilderness and my heart was full of love and gratitude.

Over the years, I have kept a gratitude journal on and off. They have contained big events like cars, new apartments and promotions, but mostly the simple mundane things of life like the joy of taking a nap, exercising, moments with the wonderful people in my life, easy commutes and great meals. Keeping that journal connects me with what's true in my life: all my needs are met in each moment, I have joy and friendship and I am loved. It connects me with my source, my God. In each moment, I appreciate all that I have been and am given. I savor life and possessions in a way I could never have imagined before my misfortune.

I filed for bankruptcy in November 1995, and in this moment I can finally say to you without reservation or pause that I see the perfection in what happened to me. There wasn't any other path that could have brought me to this moment. Any other choice years ago would have brought me to another point, good or bad, right or wrong, but not this exact spot. And, in my acceptance of

all that I've been through, there is both love and gratitude.

I am grateful I didn't quit or give up on my life. I am
grateful I can appreciate the gift of a coffee mug from
my local dry cleaner after an unexpectedly long wait. I
treasure it as it was hand painted and I could tell she
gave it to me from her heart. So my heart accepted it. I'm
grateful when I see a homeless person and see myself in
them, a recognition that we are all one. I am grateful for
the lovely view of God's great earth, especially the
mountains. The joy of a young nephew cupping my
cheek in his hand is immeasurable. And, I adore enjoying laughter and camaraderie with friends. These are my
sweet victories, greater than any possessions.

The abundance I now enjoy gives me breathing
room and options. I can experience the joy of spending
time with family because I have the money to take the
trip, and laughter with my friends as I drive an hour in
my lovely car to see them. I have breathing room with
my bills, thanks to a comfortable salary and money in
my savings account. I have choices now that I didn't
have when I had less than enough. There is freedom
with abundance and I create that freedom every day
with my thoughts and feelings.

There did come a time when I had to ask myself,
"How much is enough?" How much money and how
many possessions will make up for my losses? How
much was I willing to work for? I have always had the
goal of becoming a millionaire, but as I approached a
six-figure income, contentment set in. I had three weeks
of vacation a year at my job. I had more time than I

could fill constructively. I am a good steward of God's money, which has afforded me the right to trust that all my needs are met. So, how much is enough? I don't yet have all the money and time to do what I could to make this a better world, to help more people who have experienced similar failures or challenges in their lives. I don't have enough to provide college scholarships to give people a shot at changing the world for the better.

As I ponder the question, "How much is enough?" my answer is, "Enough to make a difference." Oprah Winfrey is a role model for making a difference. She builds homes and schools and sponsors organizations doing amazing work both in the US and abroad.

I recently read a new expanded definition of wealth that also answers the question, "How much is enough?" It's from a book entitled *The Maui Millionaires* (Wiley, 2007). Authors David Finkel and Diane Kennedy discuss six main areas of wealth:

a. "Financial Wealth: your financial net worth, passive cash flow, active cash flow and financial prospects.

b. Emotional Wealth: self-understanding, acceptance, and love; satisfying and healthy relationships with other people; and sense of joy and happiness.

c. Spiritual Wealth: a satisfying connection to a deeper meaning or higher power; a sense of fulfilling your life's purpose; peace of mind.

d. Physical Wealth: a feeling of vitality, energy, and physical well-being.

e.   Intellectual Wealth: a sense of curiosity and eagerness for learning; intellectual growth and positive challenges.

f.   Time Wealth: a feeling of abundance of time in your life; a healthy balance between all areas of your life."

The "Maui Millionaires" believe that to be truly wealthy you must be wealthy in all six areas. A big part of their mission is to also give back and make a difference in the world by creating foundations and supporting charities.

I may not have made it to millionaire status yet, but I am already looking for ways to help others. That's why I wrote this book. I am so grateful for all that I've learned on this journey, I simply have to share.

Your Journey

1. What are you grateful for today? Even if it was a challenging day, you can be grateful for your breathing, for it is your gift to yourself. You can be grateful for your beating heart, even if it feels broken. Name at least three things you are grateful for:

2. Have you thought about how much is enough? When I was making less than $20,000 a year, $50,000 seemed like a good place to be. When I got to $50,000, I set my sights on $100,000 but believed for $70,000. Knowing that you can change it any time you want, write a believable income target that would bring you great joy if you reached it:

3. If you got a check in the mail tomorrow for that exact amount, what would you do?

I encourage you to start a daily gratitude journal to take note of the blessings you already have in your life. If you are already keeping a gratitude journal, add 2-3 additional items to be grateful for each day. As you increase your awareness of what you are grateful for, more will flow to you.

———●◆●———

SUCCESS ON YOUR OWN TERMS

I am so grateful and honored that you've taken this journey with me. And now, it's time to more clearly define your own *journey to abundance* and what you want to experience along the way.

Success is in how one thinks and feels about their lives. Abundance or poverty is in the words they say or meditate on. A person can feel successful or poor whether they are making $10,000 a year or $10,000 a month. Success is more about who you are, your character and integrity, than what you do or what you have. Have you defined what success is to you? Not by anyone else's definition, just your own?

I am not yet a millionaire, although it is a desire. I don't live in a mansion, but I live comfortably. I am not a CEO, but I work at a level that allows me the time and energy to do other things that are important to me. By my own definition, I am successful.

The exercises that follow are designed to move you further along your journey. Take time to answer each question. Be fully honest with yourself, leave out what you think you "should" want, and go for what you truly, truly desire. Have fun and dream big!

Your Journey

1. What is your definition of success? Write it here:

2. Beyond having abundance and peace, success is also about living on purpose, using your talents and abilities to do that thing that makes your heart sing. How are you living your life's purpose today?

3. If you are not sure what your life's purpose is, let me ask you this: When you were 6 or 7 years old, what did you want to be? What were you good at?

4. What do people say that you are a natural at? When do you lose track of all time and space? What would you be doing with your time if you had all the money in the world? What would you do if you knew you couldn't fail? What is your heart's greatest desire?

For me, I was always helping people solve their problems. I seemed to have come into this world with a knowing that helped me see possibilities in others that they couldn't see for themselves. Of course, it was easier to see for them than for myself. And, now I am taking steps in my life to live more fully in helping others.

5. What is stopping you from moving in the direction of your wildest dream? Fear, lack of money, lack of time, competing commitments, lack of clarity as to what to do next, lack of faith that you could do it, lack of support, someone told you that you couldn't or shouldn't, or something else? Write down any and all of these fears or situations. By writing them down and getting them out of your head, their energy will begin to dissipate. You will have more power over them than they will have over you.

6. Would you be willing to spend a few minutes a day for the next three days daydreaming about the possibility of following your heart's desire? Yes/No.

7. Let's start now. For the next five minutes, close your eyes and see yourself living your life's purpose, whatever it is. Go ahead, I give you permission to dream. Really get into it. See yourself in that situa-

tion living the life of your dreams. See how all of your needs are met; see yourself peaceful, joyful and abundant while doing the thing you feel called to do. Describe your visualization in great detail:

8. Did your visualization include experiences you would like to have in your life? What is a believable income target for you?

9. Where would you like to live? What type of home would you like to have?

10. What accolades or recognition would you like to receive?

11. Describe the quality of your family relationships or how you spend your time. Add more of these details below. Remember to be as descriptive as possible, using all of your senses to describe the life of your dreams.

12. What will your new possessions feel like to touch?

13. How does the air outside of your new home smell?

14. What do you hear outside of your window?

15. Take a moment now to review your earlier list from the exercise in "Dream Big" on pages 56-57. Is there anything else you would like to experience, including trips or other material possessions? What would you like to learn, like skydiving, a foreign language or martial arts? As you start living the life of your dreams, you can continue to come back to this section to cross off things you've done and add the new adventures you would like to live. Keep dreaming and add in any new goals here:

16. What did that exercise feel like for you? Are you smiling just thinking about your dream life? Or, was it scary and seemed too far off and unbelievable? Relax and remember, we are still just playing.

17. Write a list of things you'd like to accomplish in the next one-year, two-year or even five-year period:

18. What could you do in the next couple of days that could move you in the direction of your life's purpose? Remember that you are not committing to anything just yet; let's just start brainstorming.

Here are some possibilities:

- ✓ Research the Internet or visit your public library;
- ✓ Make a call to find out more information;
- ✓ Call a friend for support or brainstorming;
- ✓ Write a letter to yourself of what it would be like a year from now if you were living your dream;
- ✓ Interview someone who is already doing what you would like to do;

Okay, now it's time to make a commitment. Review your answers from the exercises throughout the book, especially your priorities and action steps from the "Do Over" chapter on pages 40-41.

19. What can you commit to over the next 24-72 hours? Is it one of the actions you brainstormed above? Or will you start how I did, simply by saying word "wealth" over and over again for a few minutes first thing in the morning and/or before you go to bed. Saying "wealth" is a way to feel what it would be like to be at the next level in your life, whether that's an extra $50 a week or an extra $5,000, $50,000 or more in your savings account. Wherever you are and whatever you choose is perfect for you. Write down what you can realistically be counted on to complete.

To avoid overwhelm, write down no more than five items. No shoulds on this list! The goal is to boost your confidence, experience success, and create momentum.

20. Look at your list. Commit from your heart to what you are willing to and can be counted on to do for yourself. Above all, be kind to yourself and don't over commit. Revise your list here as necessary.

21. Next, write down WHY you want to take each of the actions listed above, and how it will make you feel to complete it. Adding the why and the feeling will help propel you toward completing each item, build

momentum and move you toward the life of your dreams.

With your action steps, whys and feelings now written, how can you best support yourself in following through on your commitments? Personally, I sometimes use additional methods to ensure my success, such as a timer and rewards.

For instance, if I need to straighten up an area of my living environment, do some writing, or make a call that just needs to be made, I will set the timer for 15 minutes and do as much as I can in that timeframe. I give myself the freedom to quit when the bell sounds. However, just by getting started I usually create enough momentum to keep working and complete these necessary tasks.

I also use rewards like allowing myself to watch a television show, take a walk or call a friend once the task is complete. Set your environment up for you to win!

22. Write down a few rewards that might assist you in taking action. They don't have to cost any money, they just have to inspire you to go for your dreams.

"Do that which is before you," is a phrase I learned from Reverend Diane. When I was stuck, I would hear that phrase within me and my intuition would guide me as to the next step to take, whether it was to make a call, pay a bill, or do some visualization and writing about what I want to manifest in my life. And, I'd follow through, one step at a time. There may be times ahead when you continue to say to yourself, "I don't know what to do." Please come back and revisit this book whenever you need to and "do that which is before you."

Take a minute to go back through this book and glance at all that you have written. If you have done even one exercise, applaud yourself. If you have completed most or all, give yourself a standing ovation ending with a high five. To be willing to do this work takes great courage.

———◆◆✕◆———

BLESSINGS FOR YOUR JOURNEY

My friend, thank you for taking this journey with me. You've seen where I've been and where I've come to—a place of peace, joy and abundance. I know that I am a master manifestor and I now choose to manifest carefully and consciously. I learned the truth of the saying, "Be careful what you wish for, because you just might get it." I only want to manifest those things that will bring me more peace, joy and abundance, and are for the highest good of all concerned. I want to live in harmony with myself and all that is around me. My wish is for you to experience greater peace, joy and abundance for yourself, no matter where you are in your life now and in the future.

Wherever you are in this moment is just where you are now. You can be wherever you want to be, if you move in the direction of your wildest dream. If you have always put others before yourself, start today and make yourself a priority. If you are living the life you desire, your cup will be full. You will be happier and more fulfilled and you will be able to share more of yourself.

Dream big for yourself and that will empower those around you to dream big for themselves. I give you permission to dream a better life and lifestyle, to experience luxury, to have peace and love abound in your heart and in your relationships, and to experience abundance in all areas of your life. You are a gift to this world and we need you to fully share your talents and abilities. We need you to live the life you were meant to live, so that all of us can grow to a greater place of awareness. I believe in you and have faith that you can move forward along your chosen path. Why? Because I'm doing it and if I can, anyone can.

I encourage you to write me and let me know your story and your progress towards living an abundant life. And if you have completed all of the exercises in this book, definitely let me know. I have a special gift for you. Until then and always, you are in my thoughts and prayers.

Blessings for a joyful, abundant journey,
Kamin

APPENDIX A: FORGIVENESS LETTER

Dear_____

Date_____

I am writing this letter to share my feelings.

1.   For ANGER
I don't like it . . . . . .
I feel frustrated . . . . . .
I am angry that . . . . . .
I feel annoyed . . . . . .
I want . . . . . .

2.   For SADNESS
I feel disappointed . . . . . .
I am sad that . . . . . .
I feel hurt . . . . . .
I wanted . . . . . .
I want . . . . . .

3.   For FEAR
I feel worried . . . . . .
I am afraid . . . . . .

I feel scared . . . . . .
I do not want . . . . . .
I need . . . . . .
I want . . . . . .

4.   For REGRET
I feel embarrassed . . . . . .
I am sorry . . . . . .
I feel ashamed . . . . . .
I didn't want . . . . . .
I want . . . . . .

5.   For LOVE AND FORGIVENESS
I love . . . . . .
I want . . . . . .
I understand . . . . . .
I forgive . . . . . .
I appreciate . . . . . .
I thank you for . . . . . .
I know . . . . . .

P.S. The response I would like to hear from you:

APPENDIX B: RESOURCES

I have chosen a few of my favorite books about abundance, prosperity and success that helped me along my journey.

5 Gifts for an Abundant Life by Diane Harmony. Universal Harmony House: 2003.

21-Day Countdown to Success by Chris Witting. Career Press: 1998

Absolutely Effortless Prosperity, Revised Edition by Bijan Anjomi. Effortless Prosperity Inc.: 1997.

The Abundance Book by John Randolph Price. Hay House: 2005.

Acres of Diamonds by Russell H. Conwell. Bnpublishing.com: 2007.

The Aladdin Factor by Jack Canfield, Mark Victor Hansen. Berkley Trade: 1995.

As a Man Thinketh by James Allen. Willside Press: 2005.

As a Woman Thinketh by Dorothy Hulst. Lushena Books: 2000

Ask And It Is Given: Learning To Manifest Your Desires by Esther Hicks, Jerry Hicks, Wayne W. Dyer (Foreword). Hay House: 2004.

Attracting Perfect Customers by Stacey Hall and Jan Brogniez. Berrett-Koehler Publishers: 2001.

The Attractor Factor by Joe Vitale. John Wiley & Sons: 2001.

Awaken the Giant Within: How to Take Immediate Control of Your Mental, Emotional, Physical, and Financial by Anthony Robbins. Free Press: 1992

Building Your Field of Dreams by Mary Manin Morrissey. Bantam: 1997.

Busting Loose From the Money Game by Robert Scheinfeld. Wiley: 2006.

Change Your Thoughts - Change Your Life: Living the Wisdom of the Tao (Hardcover) by Wayne W. Dyer. Hay House: 2007.

Creating Money: Keys to Abundance (Life Mastery Series) by Sanaya Roman, Duane Packer. HJ Kramer: 1988.

Creating True Prosperity by Shakti Gawain. New World Library, Nataraj: 2000.

Divine Intuition by Lynn Robinson. DK ADULT: 2001.

The Dynamic Laws of Prosperity by Catherine Ponder. DeVorss & Company: 1985.

Expressing Your Feelings by Roger T. Crenshaw, M.D. Irvington Pub: 1981.

Finding Your True Calling by Valerie Young. Changing Course: 2002.

Get The Edge – CD by Anthony Robbins. 2000.

The Greatest Salesman in the World by Og Mandino. Bantam: 1983.

Guilt Is the Teacher, Love Is the Lesson by Joan Borysenko. HarperCollins Publishers Ltd: 1993.

It Works by R.H. Jarrett. DeVorss & Company: 1976.

The Law of Attraction: The Basics of the Teachings of Abraham by Esther Hicks and Jerry Hicks. Hay House: 2006.

The Magic of Believing by Claude M. Bristol. Pocket: 1991.

The Magic of Thinking Big by David Schwartz. Simon & Schuster: 1987.

Making a Living Without a Job: Winning Ways For Creating Work That You Love by Barbara Winter. Bantam: 1993.

The Maui Millionaires by Diane Kennedy and David Finkel. John Wiley & Sons: 2007.

Money Is My Friend by Phil Laut. Ballantine Books: 1999.

Open Your Mind to Prosperity by Catherine Ponder. DeVorss & Company: 1984.

The Passion Test by Janet Bray Attwood and Chris Attwood. Hudson Street Press: 2007.

The Power of Intention by Wayne W. Dyer. Hay House: 2005.

The Power of Focus by Jack Canfield, Mark Victor Hansen, and Les Hewitt. Vermilion: 2001.

The Power of Your Subconscious Mind, Revised Edition by Joseph Murphy. Bantam: 1982.

Real Prosperity: Using the Power of Intuition to Create Financial and Spiritual Abundance by Lynn Robinson. Andrews McMeel Publishing: 2004.

A Return to Love by Marianne Williamson. Harper Paperbacks: 1996.

Richest Man in Babylon by George S. Clason. Signet: 2004.

The Secret by Rhonda Byrne. Atria Books/Beyond
     Words: 2006.
Secrets of the Millionaire Mind by T. Harv Eker. Collins:
     2005.
*The Seven Spiritual Laws of Success: A Practical Guide to
     the Fulfillment of Your Dreams (based on Creating Af-
     fluence)* by Deepak Chopra. Amber-Allen Publish-
     ing: 2007.
Simple Abundance: A Daybook of Comfort of Joy by Sarah
     Ban Breathnach. Grand Central Publishing: 1995.
The Success Principles by Jack Canfield and Janet
     Switzer. Collins: 2006.
Think and Grow Rich by Napoleon Hill. Aventine Press:
     2004.
*Unlimited Power: The New Science Of Personal Achieve-
     ment* by Anthony Robbins. Free Press: 1997.
*You'll See It When You Believe It: The Way to Your
     Personal Transformation* by Wayne W. Dyer. Harper
     Paperbacks: 2001.
Your Heart's Desire by Sonia Choquette. Three Rivers
     Press: 1997.
You've GOT to Read this Book! by Jack Canfield and Gay
     Hendricks. Collins: 2006.
*Women & Money: Owning the Power to Control Your
     Destiny* by Suze Orman. Spiegel & Grau: 2007.

APPENDIX C: TIMELINE OF SIGNIFICANT EVENTS

June 1985	Entered the Navy
March 1992	Masters in Information Systems
March 1993	Joined the sales organization
September 1994	Left the Navy
November 1995	Declared bankruptcy
March 1996	Bankruptcy discharged (finalized by the court)
August 1996	Left the sales organization
August 1996	Started working for the doctor
December 1997	Started web development on doctor's website
April 1998	Created "Quick Computing for Women" software program
August 1999	Began working for computer company
June 2002	Credit & FICO score restored
June 2002	Manifested dream car
August 2004	Manifested dream apartment
August 2005	Received Masters of Arts in Spiritual Psychology from University of Santa Monica

Permissions

Finkel, David and Diane Kennedy (2007). *The Maui Millionaires*. New Jersey: John Wiley and Sons. Reprinted with permission of John Wiley & Sons, Inc.

Harmony, Diane (2004). *5 Gifts for an Abundant Life*. California: Universal Harmony House. Reprinted with permission of Universal Harmony House.

Murphy, Joseph (1982). *The Power of Your Subconscious Mind*. New York: Bantam; Reissue edition. All rights reserved.

Ponder, Catherine (1985). *The Dynamic Laws of Prosperity*. California: DeVorss & Company. Reprinted with permission of DeVorss Publications.

Winter, Barbara J. (1993). *Making a Living Without a Job: Winning Ways For Creating Work That You Love*. New York: Bantam. All rights reserved.

The American Heritage® Dictionary. Massachusetts. Houghton Mifflin Company, 1982.

Notes

Notes

Notes

Notes

ABOUT THE AUTHOR

Kamin Bell knows about manifesting heart's desires. She started her professional career as the U.S. Navy's first female African-American helicopter pilot. She then went on to become a Mary Kay Sales Director and consultant. Kamin's next desire was to learn the Web and has been working on the Internet in various capacities for over 10 years.

Kamin holds a Masters of Science in Computer Systems and realized a twenty-year dream when she received a Masters of Arts in Spiritual Psychology in 2005.

Kamin is passionate about helping people attract more abundance into their lives and achieve their dreams and desires. She has helped numerous people connect to their ideal life, create a plan to live their life on purpose and realize their dreams.

To learn more about Kamin Bell and her programs, please visit www.kaminbell.com.

Printed in the United States
97365LV00005B/2/A

9 780980 022322